This Book Donated by

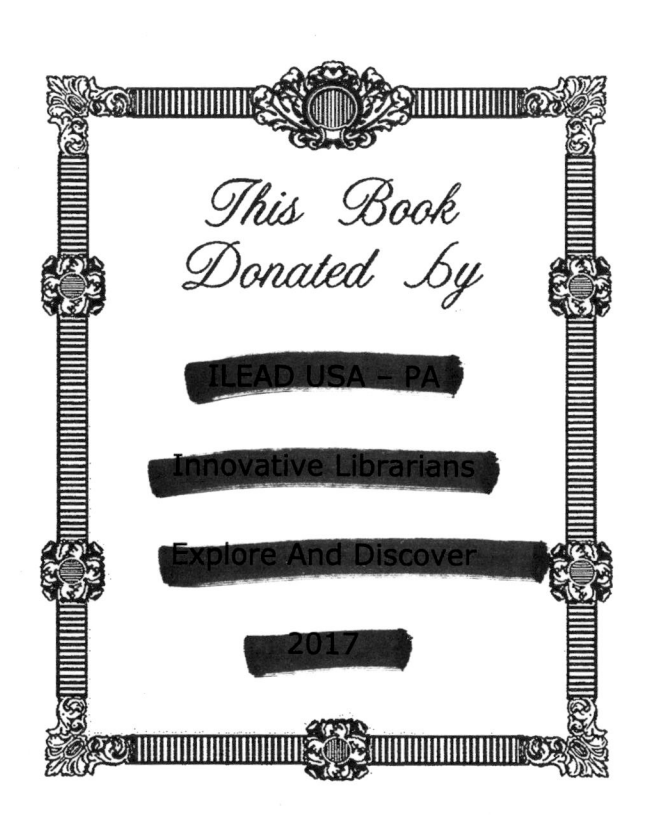

ILEAD USA – PA

Innovative Librarians

Explore And Discover

2017

MEDIA LITERACY™

DIGITAL CONTENT CREATION

MEGAN FROMM, Ph.D.

rosen publishing's
rosen central®

NEW YORK

Published in 2015 by The Rosen Publishing Group, Inc.
29 East 21st Street, New York, NY 10010

Copyright © 2015 by Megan Fromm

First Edition

All rights reserved. No part of this book may be reproduced in any form without permission in writing from the publisher, except by a reviewer.

Library of Congress Cataloging-in-Publication Data

Fromm, Megan.
Digital content creation/Megan Fromm.—First edition.
    pages cm.—(Media literacy)
Includes bibliographical references and index.
ISBN 978-1-4777-8060-2 (library bound)
1. Online journalism—Juvenile literature. I. Title.
PN4784.O62F76 2015
808'.06607—dc23

2014009350

Manufactured in Malaysia

CONTENTS

4 INTRODUCTION

6 CHAPTER ONE
ONLINE-ONLY PUBLICATIONS

16 CHAPTER TWO
EDITING DIGITAL CONTENT:
A PROFILE OF DARLA CAMERON

20 CHAPTER THREE
HYPERLOCAL NEWS

27 CHAPTER FOUR
WORKING ON THE HOMEPAGE:
A PROFILE OF DORIS TRUONG

30 CHAPTER FIVE
THE CHALLENGES OF ONLINE
COMMUNITIES

35 CHAPTER SIX
WORKING AS A JOURNALIST:
A PROFILE OF DAN LAMOTHE

Glossary 39
For More Information 40
For Further Reading 43
End Notes 44
Index 46

INTRODUCTION

When it comes to websites, distinguishing between traditional news organizations, blogs, news aggregators, and personal websites is not as easy as it seems. Traditional news sites often revamp their design and function to compete with social sites, and even personal bloggers can create news templates that look (and perhaps are) strikingly professional in nature.

Today's journalists function almost entirely in a virtual, online world, so citizens must learn to navigate this digital information landscape without getting lost along the way. And while digital natives—those who have grown up in the age of the Internet—may feel well versed in the language of the World Wide Web, the ever-changing pace of technology is hard to match.

To better understand what role a website is trying to fill (information, entertainment, commentary), consider first how the site is structured, what purpose the site (and the information it presents) intends to serve, and who is working behind the scenes. By comparing and contrasting the qualities found in traditional news formats to those used in online mediums, citizens can become better aware of the variety of platforms and content available today.

INTRODUCTION

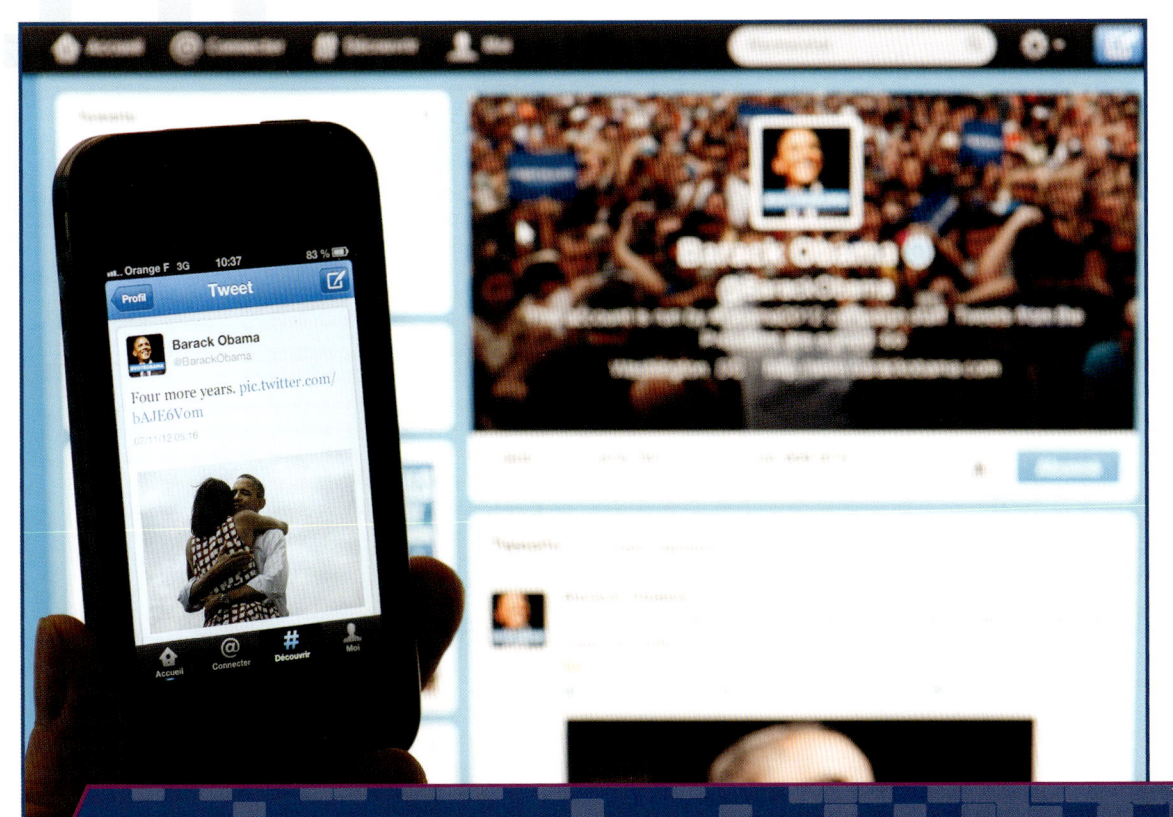

When President Barack Obama won reelection in 2012, his "Four More Years" tweet was shared across social media 472,000 times in three hours.

    In fact, building this kind of digital knowledge database is essential repertoire in media literacy education because it requires consumers to know enough to ask insightful questions, make value judgments, and analyze media for themselves. In developing an expertise in the digital landscape, citizens are empowered to make choices that reflect critical thinking instead of knee-jerk responses to the latest trending story.

    But simply being exposed to online media is not enough to cultivate digital fluency. Despite growing up surrounded by media and technology, digital natives do not simply learn to be critical consumers via osmosis. Recognizing how news platforms operate online, the typical structures of media, and what contemporary journalism jobs look like are ideal first steps into active digital citizenship.

CHAPTER ONE

ONLINE-ONLY PUBLICATIONS

In the last decade, many news organizations have transitioned to operating fully online. That means they no longer print a physical newspaper or news magazine. Some of these publications include major newspapers like the *Seattle Post-Intelligencer* and newsmagazines like *Newsweek*. Others represent new genres of journalism and amorphous blends of traditional and new media.

While the economic realities of these transitions are explored later, let's look at two major online-only publications that represent current trends in journalism.

ONLINE-ONLY PUBLICATIONS

In their New York City office, ProPublica staffers celebrate winning a Pulitzer Prize for the second year in a row.

PROPUBLICA

ProPublica, an independent online news site that has only ever existed digitally, is a perfect example of a hybrid organization that blurs the lines between traditional, investigative journalism and online blog. In fact, the website in 2011 won the first Pulitzer Prize awarded for stories that were never published in print.[1]

With a catchphrase of "journalism in the public interest," ProPublica even offers some of its deep investigative work to other publications free of

DIGITAL CONTENT CREATION

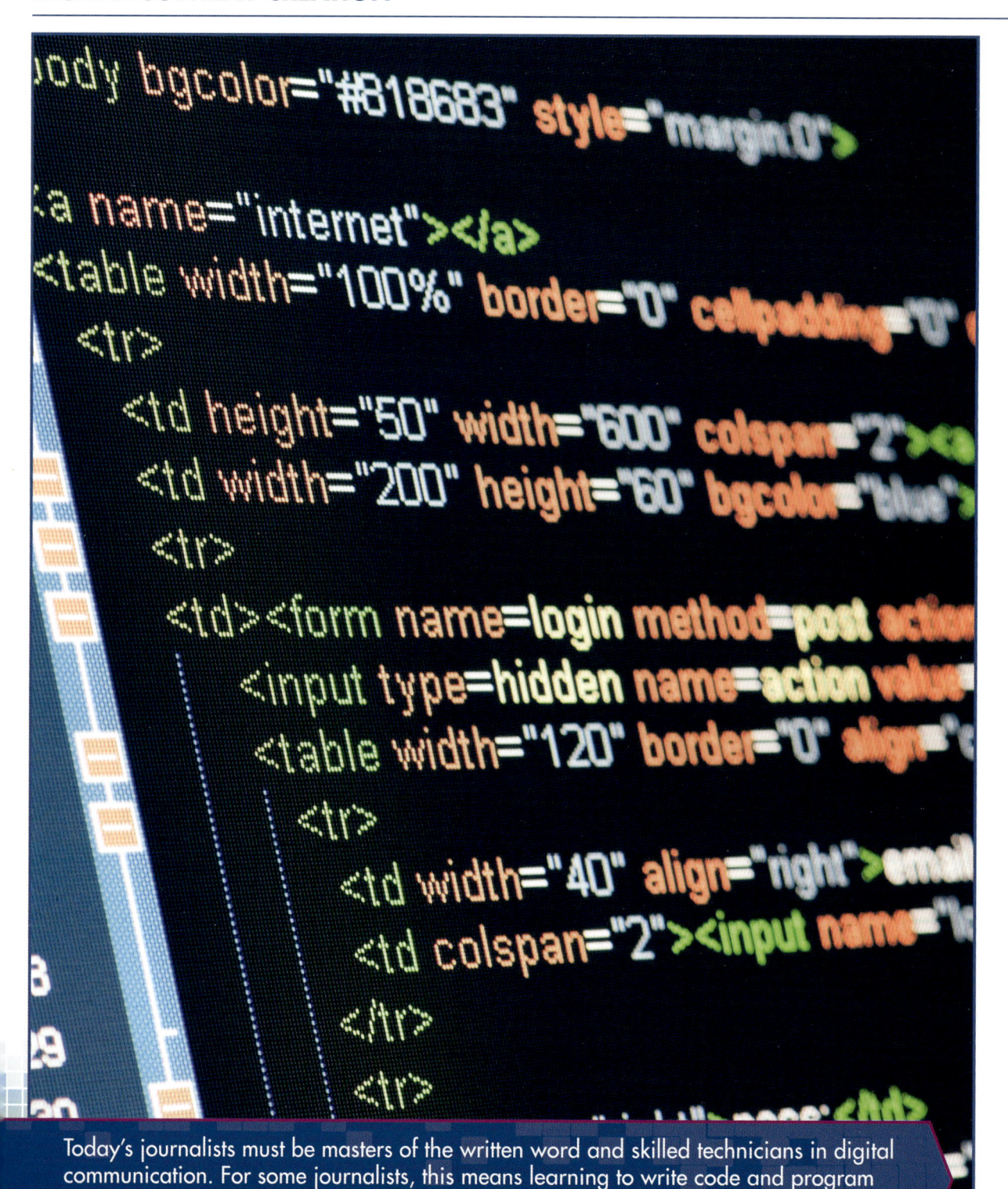

Today's journalists must be masters of the written word and skilled technicians in digital communication. For some journalists, this means learning to write code and program web pages.

charge. While some critics have dubbed the publication a blog, the organization describes itself as a group of highly trained journalists focused on investigative reporting for one simple reason: "In short, we face a situation in which sources of opinion are proliferating, but sources of *facts* on which those *opinions* are based are shrinking."[2]

In January 2014, ProPublica had about forty dedicated staffers covering beats such as education, terrorism, the military, and the environment.

SLATE

Other online-only publications are less "traditional" in the sense that their goal is not exclusively news. Rather, they have a more balanced, integrated mix of columnists, editorials, entertainment pieces, interactive pieces, and news stories. Slate is one example of this hybrid, online-only publication. Visit Slate's homepage and you'll find articles on a presidential campaign displayed side by side with commentary on which Olympic athletes are posing for advertisers and sponsors.

In fact, Slate hosts its own forum of bloggers who write about everything from sports to money to culture. The publication also prides itself on its social media presence, an area of audience relations that many traditional newspapers are just now exploring. Most of Slate's staffers are experienced and well-respected journalists, many of whom spend significant time throughout their careers working on longer, investigative pieces that tackle major political or cultural issues.

THE PUSH FOR CODE

Both ProPublica and Slate still have relatively traditional staffing structures, including reporters, graphics and visual editors, copy editors, and senior managing editors. However, instead of page layout and designers, these online-only publications have web developers and coders who can help ensure content is visualized correctly in an online space.

DIGITAL CONTENT CREATION

Online newspapers often rely on web developers to be sure that website content appears accurately and in a visually appealing way.

ONLINE-ONLY PUBLICATIONS

Interestingly, traditional page designers for print publications were often graduates of journalism schools or those with training akin to a professional reporter. So, when news copy left the reporter's hands and was ready to be designed—or laid out—in the publication space, it was usually still a "typical" journalist handling the material.

Now, web developers and coders often come from technical and engineering backgrounds instead of journalism school. This generally has little bearing on how news copy is handled on a website, but the influx into the journalism field of professionals who may have little journalism training is a relatively new phenomenon.

Because of this shift and the desire to preserve the role of a journalist, many

DIGITAL CONTENT CREATION

JOURNALISTS AND CODE

HTML. CSS. CGI. DBMS. If you don't understand these acronyms, then you likely are not a web developer or coder. But if you're a journalist, perhaps that shouldn't matter. As more and more publications move online, the need for journalists to be technologically proficient in web design and programming skills is ever greater.

In fact, many journalism critics—and professional journalists themselves—argue that students should skip journalism school and instead learn more about information technology, programming, and website development. Without these skills, they say, journalists will be unmarketable in the near future.

PBS even went so far as to say those journalists who wish to be working in the industry into the next decade must learn coding.[3] But why? Simply put, it bridges the

Web programming ranges from simple, build-it-yourself templates to intricate code. Many publishers now believe all journalists should have some background in coding.

ONLINE-ONLY PUBLICATIONS

> gap between the story (the facts, context, angle) and presentation (how it visually appears on a website), including how fast it loads, whether it's readable and user friendly, and what supplementary visual content accompanies it. Master coders, such as those currently using layering technology with HTML5, know that code is a gateway for creating more interactive, engaging online articles.

journalists and journalism educators are calling for every journalist to learn basic coding skills.

Knowing how to program a story virtually, as opposed to designing that story on a physical newspaper spread, can also mean journalists develop a keener sense of how their story fits into larger contextual issues or geophysical aspects. Coding allows journalists to intrinsically link one story with another, or one data set with multiple maps or documents. Because of this, the inherent options of web building also force journalists to consider all possible connections between their story and other content. This can result in deeper, more meaningful coverage.

SOLO JOURNALISTS

Some journalists skip the newsroom community altogether, opting to publish one-person operations. Because technology is becoming lighter and more portable, the idea of a "backpack journalist"—one who carries all the necessary reporting and publishing gear as he or she travels—is common.

In 2005, Yahoo! correspondent Kevin Sites became one of the most well-known backpack journalists when he spent a year traveling to every major conflict zone in the world. Using only the gear he had on him and occasional access to translators, Sites published photos, videos, and stories

DIGITAL CONTENT CREATION

Kevin Sites *(right)* was an embedded journalist in Fallujah, Iraq, in 2004. Sites has visited dozens of armed conflict zones around the world, documenting war using only a backpack full of technology.

ONLINE-ONLY PUBLICATIONS

from dozens of "hot zones" that typically receive little traditional media attention.

Today, the idea of a backpack journalist is so popular that some universities are even devoting course time to teaching students how to better operate as solo journalists. American University and the University of North Carolina at Pembroke are just two of many universities and colleges that recognize the need to teach students how to report independently with limited resources and emerging technology.

Backpack journalists have the distinct advantage of traveling lightly and are often entrenched in a local community, making contact with reliable sources and developing a keen awareness of what's important and relevant to their audience. This kind of on-the-spot reporting makes backpack journalists a unique breed of reporters who use their proximity to events to leverage readership.

CHAPTER TWO

EDITING DIGITAL CONTENT:
A PROFILE OF DARLA CAMERON

Employer: The *Washington Post*
Position: Interactive graphics editor
Education: University of Missouri, bachelor of journalism, 2008

Past journalism experience:
I was a news artist at the *Tampa Bay Times* (formerly the *St. Petersburg Times*) for four years before joining the *Post* in 2013. Before I began my career, I was a busy student journalist in high school and college, when I worked at the *Columbia Missourian* and the *Maneater* student newspaper and completed internships at *Tulsa World* and *Grand Junction Daily Sentinel*.

Did you work in student media in high school or college? If so, how did that prepare you for your current career?
My first and best journalism teacher was Mark Newton, the adviser of my high school student newspaper. I'm a journalist because he taught me

to love telling stories. At the University of Missouri, I worked for the student newspaper and university-run city newspaper and gained invaluable experience—both were environments where it was OK to make mistakes and learn from them. My interests in journalism evolved as I went through school and worked as a student journalist—when I started college, I wanted to be a writer, but I quickly realized how much fun it is to tell visual stories with graphics. I wouldn't have made that realization in a class—real-world journalism experience is so important. I also completed a fellowship at the Poynter Institute, a journalism school in Florida, which challenged me to think critically about my work and taught the importance of teamwork.

Describe a typical "day in your life" at your current job.
My days are usually determined by the news. I attend daily meetings on the *Post*'s financial desk, and sometimes I make graphics responding to the business news of the day, whether that's analyzing Twitter's initial public-offering plans or making a map to show housing sales data. To find data for a graphic, I enlist help from a reporter or data analyst on the *Post*'s graphic desk, or I call sources myself to request information. Once I have data, I open it up in Microsoft Excel or Adobe Illustrator, a drawing program, to see what it shows and find out what shape a graphic might take. Then, I use development tools such as JavaScript and CSS to develop and design an interactive graphic. I'm also in close contact with reporters and editors about future projects, and the process for producing those is the same.

How do you find story ideas?
I use data analysis to identify the trends and patterns that support stories, but I have to know what to look for. For that, I work closely with reporters who are experts on their beats and can help me find the patterns to follow. I also pay close attention to public-policy organizations, financial services, and economic think tanks to help me understand the issues so I can explain

them clearly to readers. Graphics tell visual stories, so I'm also always looking for new and creative ways to display data online.

How do you find the right sources?
Finding source materials for graphics can be more difficult than source material for stories. As a rule, we don't draw something we didn't see, so some of our artists travel as far as war zones to get the story. It's also not enough to trace a pie chart—we have to get the data behind the chart and draw it ourselves. We often check our sources' math on different topics. It's very easy to lie with numbers and charts, and we want to hold ourselves and sources to high standards of accuracy.

Tell us about a story or project that was especially meaningful for you or your publication.
The government shutdown was one of the biggest stories of 2013 for the *Washington Post*. For three weeks, most government workers went without a paycheck while Congress decided how to pay the country's bills. The *Post* graphics department worked nearly around the clock to show how the government pays its debt, track the impact of the shutdown, categorize lawmakers' political motives, and more. It was an exhilarating and exhausting time to be a journalist, and we helped make a complex and difficult story clearer for our readers.

How do you keep up with changing technology and its impact on journalism?
The technology and tools we use to do journalism have changed drastically even during my relatively short career. When I started college, we didn't worry much about getting graphics onto the web. By the time I graduated, Flash was the tool of choice for making interactive graphics online. Now, we use front-end code languages like JavaScript and CSS. I'm lucky to work on a team of brilliant developers, and we learn together by sharing new tools and techniques that we find online.

EDITING DIGITAL CONTENT: A PROFILE OF DARLA CAMERON

What role do you think citizens have to play in being engaged and critical of the information they consume?
Data journalism and graphics provide context for the news, which can help back up whether a news report is accurate or false. Accurately presented numbers don't lie, and data can make stories more credible or show when a trend is not true.

What advice do you have for students interested in media and journalism careers?
This is the most exciting time to be a journalist. The business of media is changing every day, and that means we get to adapt and find new ways to tell stories online. Don't be afraid of computer programming and code—data can help you find and tell amazing stories.

Is there anything else you'd like to add?
As my high school journalism adviser told us: Go big or go home!

CHAPTER THREE

HYPERLOCAL NEWS

While state and regional news publications flounder under immense economic uncertainty, some journalists and corporations are turning to local news to seek out profits and drive readership. By turning to hyperlocal news, corporations are hoping to distinguish themselves from the aggregated mass news that's available online.

Hyperlocal news focuses on discrete, specific communities, often (though not always) using a small-scale business model instead of a corporate model that demands unreasonably high profit margins. However, just like their more traditional news counterparts, hyperlocal outlets must balance costs with revenue, and some ventures have yet to find the economic sweet spot.

HYPERLOCAL NEWS

AOL's Patch.com news sites provide hyperlocal news to users but have struggled to remain competitive in the online market. Hundreds of their employees were laid off in 2013.

PATCH.COM

Acquired by AOL in 2009, hyperlocal news network Patch.com is one example of how a national model for local news just may not work. Operating some 900 local news sites across 23 states, Patch sites rely on a mix of local and national advertising to support locally sourced information

DIGITAL CONTENT CREATION

As many newspapers downsize, local publishers are searching for ways to create niche markets supported by community-oriented reporting and advertising.

HYPERLOCAL NEWS

and human-interest stories. Facing multimillion-dollar deficits, Patch laid off hundreds of employees in 2013 before turning over majority ownership to investment company Hale Global in early 2014.[4] In January 2014, the new owners laid off even more employees as part of a restructuring designed to make the publication more profitable.

As *USA Today*'s Rem Rieder explains, hyperlocal news isn't the golden goose some once thought it could be: "The idea behind hyperlocal sounds entirely sensible. People like neighborhood news. Small merchants need a place in which to advertise where they can target their home audience and not pay the freight for an ad in a major metro daily. And as those dailies cut back, there's an underserved market. Problem is, as is so often the case on the Internet, there just aren't enough digital ad dollars to make the numbers work."

Contrary to their hyperlocal but nationalized counterparts, like Patch.com, truly local, independent news organizations are finding somewhat stable ground, even if their employees are overworked and underpaid. In fact, the

23

DIGITAL CONTENT CREATION

NICHE NEWS

Like hyperlocal news, niche news is also facing a rejuvenation in the digital age. Niche publications focus on a specific kind of content such as sports, politics, or culture and entertainment. In fact, in Pew Research Center's 2013 *State of the News Media* report, researchers noted that traditional news media are being subsumed in part by more topic-specific publications. Many journalists who once worked as general assignment reporters are being replaced by experts or are developing their own expertise to carve out a niche.[5]

Niche publications are covering topics like health and education with an in-depth approach. Pew's report uses Kaiser Health News—an editorially independent nonprofit health news organization—as just one example of this shift toward industry specialization.

Writing for the Nieman Journalism Lab, niche news executive Elizabeth Green describes the trend toward specialization: "Even better, subject matter expertise also seems to have a real shot at becoming self-sustaining...We have a defined audience that a defined set of foundations, donors, and sponsors want to reach—and so raising money, while always a challenge, is relatively easier."[6]

Green argues that the move toward single-subject sites and publications, especially of the nonprofit variety, is good for democracy and readers because newsmakers will be more knowledgeable about that which they cover. In turn, readers and policy makers will be better educated for the decisions they make. As the cofounder and editor of education-centric Chalkbeat.org, Green has seen firsthand how nonprofit, special-interest, community-oriented news can thrive.

As one of five key elements to Chalkbeat's stated mission, expertise is the heart of the organization and is expected of all its journalists. The organization describes this principle more in-depth on its website: "Our

HYPERLOCAL NEWS

A shift toward niche news requires journalists to become subject-matter experts in content areas such as politics, health, religion, and education.

reporters and editors care passionately about education and are committed to learning as much about it as possible. We take our jobs as information providers seriously, and so we know that we have to become as knowledgeable as we can."[7]

publishers membership group Local Independent Online News (LION) even encouraged laid-off Patch employees to start their own community publications, arguing "AOL's Patch is failing not because local news isn't a solid business, but because they're not local."[8]

TRULY LOCAL NEWS

Dylan Smith, chairman of LION and editor and publisher of TucsonSentinel.com wrote, "Local news is successful when it truly is local—historically, when newspapers and radio stations were owned by families or local partnerships, they served their communities more effectively… Local news organizations must be of their communities, not just in them to ship profits out of town. Local news must respect readers: know what they want to know, know what they need to know, and provide it quickly, accurately and comprehensively."

A nonprofit and independent publication, TucsonSentinel.com is one of roughly one hundred publications that are LION members, each of which focuses on local, independent reporting. The publication was designed to fill a gap when the local newspaper, *Tucson Citizen*, shut down in 2009 and the *Arizona Daily Star* was repeatedly downsized.

"A metropolitan area of nearly one million deserves a vital and sustainable source of news. TucsonSentinel.com sets out to be that watchdog," writes the staff on TusconSentinel.com's "About" page. The online publication is supported through donations, advertisements, and corporate philanthropy in an attempt to "stand as a model for a new journalism: online and accessible, mindful of a tradition of dedication and with an innovative future."[9]

CHAPTER FOUR

WORKING ON THE HOMEPAGE:
A PROFILE OF DORIS TRUONG

Employer: The *Washington Post*
Position: Homepage editor
Education: Missouri School of Journalism, bachelor of journalism 1998 (news-editorial with design emphasis, and a French minor)

Past journalism experience:
I have been a copy editor in various departments at the *Dallas Morning News* (1998 to 2003) and at the *Washington Post* (2003–2013).

Did you work in student media in high school or college? If so, how did that prepare you for your current career?
I caught the journalism bug during my junior year of high school, when I was accepted to the staff of the *Orange & Black* newspaper at Grand Junction High School in Colorado. I started as a reporter, and in my senior year took on the duties of managing editor. We even managed to scoop

DIGITAL CONTENT CREATION

our hometown daily a few times—a pretty big deal for a monthly publication staffed entirely by high school students.

The *O&B*'s adviser was instrumental in steering me toward a college that specialized in teaching journalism. I picked the Missouri School of Journalism, where I was on the staff of the independent paper, the *Maneater*, as well as the university's publication, the *Columbia Missourian*.

The *Missourian* was invaluable for providing hands-on training in daily journalism methods, traditional as well as emerging. We learned to calculate by hand the lengths of stories and the dimensions of photos on the page. We also trained on a variety of content management systems, which impressed potential employers. Another benefit to attending Mizzou was the invaluable network of alumni. I still rely on it today.

Describe a typical "day in your life" at your current job.
The day doesn't really stop anymore. It's a 24-7 news environment, so I'm constantly checking e-mails from the office and regularly looking at our online platforms (desktop, tablet, and mobile). We're also expected to know how stories were played in print, so I look through the dead-tree edition, too.

For the web, we don't have to rely on words to tell the story. We can tap into a variety of multimedia offerings: video, audio, interactive graphics, photo galleries, and blogs with content that might not fit in the paper. We try to serve up the most attention-worthy content, and we're constantly monitoring metrics to see whether a headline rewrite or a fresh photo might help traffic.

What ends up on the homepage is a group decision. And breaking news can mean we scrap any plans we had made.

Tell us about a story or project that was especially meaningful for you or your publication.
"Top Secret America" was an elaborate investigative report that involved nearly all our departments at the *Washington Post*. It's a piece of service journalism that was particularly well suited to an online presentation because of the interactive components.

How do you keep up with changing technology and its impact on journalism?

We can already see how much mobile is becoming the preferred choice for people to receive breaking news (especially weather and traffic reports). Mobile devices as a way to deliver news will become increasingly important because the price point to owning a smartphone is quickly becoming more affordable to the masses.

What role do you think citizens have to play in being engaged and critical of the information they consume?

It's important that everyone bring a healthy sense of skepticism to the news. Because of the demand to be first, major missteps in news judgment are occurring even from well-respected journalism outlets. As consumers of news, we need to beware anything that sounds too juicy to be true.

What advice do you have for students interested in media and journalism careers?

Try to be a specialist: Having language skills that would allow you to work in South America, the Middle East, or Asia could be particularly helpful in coming years. Other growth areas are in technology, science, and finance.

Learn a little about everything. You don't have to be the best videographer and the best photographer and the best writer and the best editor—but you should be proficient at most and excellent at one.

Start building your portfolio early. There's a low threshold to putting your content where people can find it, but try not to give your work away, either. Journalism is valuable, and people who are skilled at it should be paid for their efforts.

And network! Join professional journalism associations and/or attend their conventions. Make connections, and be sure to follow up. You never know when you'll find someone who can open a door or become a mentor.

CHAPTER FIVE

THE CHALLENGES OF ONLINE COMMUNITIES

Evolving consumer expectations are changing not only the type of news found online, but also the structures and expectations of virtual communities in which information is traded and discussed. Most online news organizations accommodate reader interaction, either in the form of story comments, discussion forums, or social media.

Reporters are now expected to engage with readers who comment on stories, and this relatively new expectation is creating a need for policy and procedures that relate directly to online reader communities. For some journalists, this interaction fuels better reporting and increased awareness of the issues about which they write. For others, however, the growing burden to keep pace with online reader feedback is increasingly difficult.

THE CHALLENGES OF ONLINE COMMUNITIES

Some publications, such as the *Atlantic*, are testing out reader-moderated comment forums in the hopes of keeping online discussions civil and relevant.

DIGITAL CONTENT CREATION

THE DECLINE OF NETIQUETTE

Netiquette, or online etiquette, is a major concern, with some publications even shutting down reader comments entirely because such forums are too often the victim of "trolls," or online users who comment only to be malevolent. In September 2013, online magazine *Popular Science* announced it was shuttering its comment forums because without consistent and significant moderation, the forums devolved into "bad science."[10]

Because many online news sites allow anonymous comments, it's easy for reader interaction to devolve into mudslinging. Netiquette promotes civil online interactions.

CNET reporter Nick Statt wrote about the decision, explaining just how volatile some Internet communities can become: "The comments section can be among the most vile of Internet cesspools, where wars are waged without regard for things like decency and civility and where oft-used 'up vote' systems keep dissenting opinions buried and the most easily digestible one-line takedowns up top," he wrote.[11]

The effects of reader contributions, especially comment systems, on a consumer's overall perspective of any given content is still unclear. But, researchers are slowly trying to piece together just how one person's online behavior can affect someone else's behavior, and in turn, perhaps, his or her overall knowledge and opinion of information.

MODERATING ONLINE COMMUNITIES

Bob Cohn, a writer for the *Atlantic*, argued that the most productive comments sections require regular moderation, a potential problem for pared-down operations or newsrooms with little budget to hire someone to play comment police.

QUANTIFYING BIAS

In 2013, researchers tried to quantify the kinds of social biases at work in the comments section of a news aggregation site by assigning "up votes" or "down votes" to certain comments and then tracking subsequent votes on those comments. Ultimately, the study showed that the next viewer of a positively rated comment was 32 percent more likely to also vote the comment positively,[12] a type of "positive herding behavior, which essentially means that users tended to jump on the up voting bandwagon, helping these comments accumulate positive ratings."[13]

"Writers or editors have to jump into the conversation to keep it on track, or to mete out justice by removing comments or even banning the worst offenders," Cohn wrote in August 2013.[14] "It's nice to think we'll just let a thousand flowers bloom; in reality the garden needs to be weeded."

He cited another study by the University of Wisconsin-Madison, also published in 2013, that found negative comments really do impact how readers perceive content—especially when related to science and technology.[15]

Given these recent findings and their own experience, editors at the *Atlantic* are currently testing a rather risky approach to moderation: letting committed, long-time readers moderate the comments of others. Whether this move represents a shift in consumer investment in online communities or a resigned relegation of journalistic control is yet to be decided.

CHAPTER SIX

WORKING AS A JOURNALIST:
A PROFILE OF DAN LAMOTHE

Employer: The *Washington Post*
Position: National Security Writer
Education: University of Maryland-College Park, master of journalism, 2007; University of Massachusetts-Amherst, bachelor of arts in journalism, 2004

Past journalism experience:
I was with *Marine Corps Times* and the *Military Times* newspaper chain from January 2008 until October 2013. I started as an entry-level editor and left as a senior writer. The highlights of my experience there were three embedded assignments in Afghanistan, spanning about four months combined between 2010 and 2012. Covering combat was a life-changing experience, and I'm glad I took the associated risks to see it firsthand and relate to the troops on a much more personal level.

DIGITAL CONTENT CREATION

I'm also proud of several national stories I broke in that time frame, especially news that then Cpl. Dakota Meyer had been nominated by the Marine Corps to become the service's first living recipient of the Medal of Honor since the Vietnam War. From October 2013 until April 2014, I was a national security writer with *Foreign Policy* magazine, whose editors I am grateful to for allowing me to break into the national media. I broke a couple exclusives while there, detailing the fight between the army and beer maker Anheuser-Busch about a Super Bowl commercial and the companies under consideration for usage in U.S. Special Operations Command's high-tech "Iron Man" suit.

Did you work in student media in high school or college? If so, how did that prepare you for your current career?

Yes, I was editor in chief of my high school newspaper, the *Comp Chronicle*, in 1999–2000. It was published about eight times a year where I attended, Chicopee Comprehensive High School in Chicopee, Massachusetts.

My college journalism experience was even more formative. The Massachusetts *Daily Collegian* at UMass was the largest college daily in New England at the time, publishing between eight and sixteen pages at the time between Monday and Friday. As a reporter there, I covered a variety of difficult and emotionally charged subjects, including crime, student deaths, campus politics, and riots and disturbances that broke out during the 2003 play-off run by the Boston Red Sox.

As a senior, I also served as managing editor of the *Collegian*, which provided me with a significant taste in handling newsroom crises and hot-button issues at the ages of twenty-one and twenty-two.

Describe a typical "day in your life" at your current job.

I cover national security and the U.S. military for the *Post*, primarily on a blog I launched called *Checkpoint*. I update it multiple times a day, while also staying in touch with sources and occasionally pitching in on print news coverage.

As a blogger, I look to provide analysis on the news of the day and interesting photos, videos, and background that readers may not otherwise see. I also track Freedom of Information Act [FOIA] requests I have filed to see when more information will become available.

How do you find story ideas?
Reading other news sources is an obvious start-quick answer. I also track news events on a calendar and look for interesting ways to tell stories that our readers will want. As I already mentioned, I also file many FOIA requests, many of which are generated when the military shares a bit of news (a commander being fired, for example), but refuses to explain why.

How do you find the right sources?
The first, obvious answer is to look for ways to reach people in the communities you are covering, rather than simply relying on public affairs officials to share their story for them. That can be done through many mediums, including phone, Twitter, and attending events where potential sources will be and introducing myself.

Tell us about a story or project that was especially meaningful for you or your publication.
I won the Major Megan McClung Award for my coverage of combat operations by U.S. Marines in Afghanistan in 2010. I spent six weeks of that year in a war zone, gathering information while regularly going on foot patrols with U.S. forces and experiencing the life they live while deployed. I was able to capture firsthand what firefights, roadside bomb attacks, and other hazards are like, and I was able to get many rough-and-tumble infantrymen to open up about their experiences.

How do you keep up with changing technology and its impact on journalism?
Any modern journalist who isn't active on social media, especially Twitter, is doing him- or herself a huge disservice. I use it regularly, both to market my own stories and to connect with individuals who can expand my understanding of a story and possibly serve as future sources.

DIGITAL CONTENT CREATION

What role do you think citizens have to play in being engaged and critical of the information they consume?

Journalism is now more interactive than it ever has been. Ten minutes after a story is published online, it can garner hundreds of comments, some from sources who were unreachable for or unwilling to be involved in the initial publication of a story. Citizens interacting with news content in that way shapes perception and delivery of follow-up stories.

What advice do you have for students interested in media and journalism careers?

Be a student of history on whatever beats you plan to cover. If you're a military journalist, for example, know the basics of each major war and the battles in them that mattered most. If you're a local crime reporter, learn what the trends have been for drug use, corruption, and other misdeeds over the previous few decades.

Also, be willing to move for your work. It's grown more and more difficult to advance a journalism career while living only in one city or town. That's even more true for anyone outside major markets like Washington, New York, and Los Angeles.

Is there anything else you'd like to add?

Being a journalist is a privilege and something not everyone with the skills to do it is afforded. I attended college with many individuals who could have been successful national journalists, had they just been given a big break. Therefore, when you get your breaks—internships, first jobs, etc.—cherish them. Run with the opportunities, and if you decide the long hours and stress are no longer worth it, move on to something else. There's no shame in that, either.

GLOSSARY

BACKPACK JOURNALIST Also called a solo journalist; a journalist who works almost entirely independently, often writing, producing, editing, and publishing his or her work via portable technology like a smartphone or laptop.

CGI Refers to common gatewayinterface, a technological mechanism for transferring data back and forth between web pages and applications.

CSS Cascading style sheets; or a type of language programmers use to tell a computer program how given information will visually appear on a website.

DBMS Database management systems are programs that help users store, manage, and extract data for different databases.

HTML Hypertext markup language is used online to make text appear in certain formats.

HTML5 Among the newest versions of HTML, this system allows web content to be structured in more visually pleasing ways, including via layers and other interactive options.

HYBRID PUBLICATION Typically an online-only publication that mixes both blogging and journalistic styles of content and presentation.

HYPERLOCAL NEWS News that focuses on a discrete, small geographical community.

MODERATOR A person (or sometimes program) responsible for approving (or censoring) online reader comments.

NETIQUETTE A term for consumer etiquette, or behavior, when online.

NICHE NEWS News that focuses on one type of content or a specific subject matter, like education or politics.

TROLL A usually anonymous web user who posts malicious, lewd, politicizing, or even offensive and obscene comments to reader forums or articles.

FOR MORE INFORMATION

American Society of News Editors
209 Reynolds Journalism Institute
Missouri School of Journalism
Columbia, MO 65211
(573) 884-2405
Website: http://www.asne.org
According to its mission statement, the American Society of News Editors is dedicated to the leadership of American journalism.

Center for Media Literacy
22837 Pacific Coast Highway, #472
Malibu, CA 90265
(310) 804-3985
Website: http://www.medialit.org
The Center for Media Literacy provides many educational resources and updated research on media literacy education.

Columbia Journalism Review
729 Seventh Avenue
Third Floor
New York, NY 10019
(212) 854-1881
Website: http://www.cjr.org
The *Columbia Journalism Review* considers itself a monitor of press across all platforms and encourages journalistic excellence as essential to a free society.

Journalism Education Association
103 Kedzie Hall
Kansas State University
Manhattan, KS 66506-1505
(866) 532-5532

FOR MORE INFORMATION

Website: http://www.jea.org
The Journalism Education Association is the largest organization for scholastic journalism teachers and scholastic media advisers. JEA's mission is to support free and responsible scholastic journalism.

Kevin Sites
Journalism and Media Studies Centre
The University of Hong Kong, Elliot Hall
Pokfulam Road, Hong Kong
Website: http://www.kevinsitesreports.com
Kevin Sites is a backpack journalist and associate professor at the University of Hong Kong.

PBS MediaShift
Public Broadcasting Service
2100 Crystal Drive
Arlington, VA 22202
(703) 739-5000
Website: http://www.pbs.org/mediashift
Sponsored by PBS, MediaShift is designed to be a "guide to the digital revolution" by tracking and commenting on changes in the media industry.

Pew Research Center State of the News Media Survey
1615 L Street NW, Suite 700
Washington, DC 20036
(202) 419-4300
Website: http://www.stateofthemedia.org
The State of the News Media Survey is conducted yearly by the Pew Research Center. The survey tracks trends in technology, readership, newsroom size, and other aspects of the journalism industry.

DIGITAL CONTENT CREATION

ProPublica
One Exchange Plaza
55 Broadway, 23rd Floor
New York, NY 10006
(212) 514-5250
Website: http://www.propublica.org
A nonprofit, independent news organization that focuses on investigative journalism, ProPublica is funded through grants and philanthropic donations.

WEBSITES

Because of the changing nature of Internet links, Rosen Publishing has developed an online list of websites related to the subject of this book. This site is updated regularly. Please use this link to access the list:

http://www.rosenlinks.com/MEDL/Digit

FOR FURTHER READING

Aimone, Logan. *NSPA Newspaper Guidebook*. Minneapolis, MN, 2009.

Bayles, Fred. *Field Guide to Covering Local News: How to Report on Cops, Courts, Schools, Emergencies and Government*. Thousand Oaks, CA: CQ Press, 2012.

Boczkowski, Pablo J., and Eugenia Mitchelstein. *The News Gap: When the Information Preferences of the Media and the Public Diverge*. Cambridge, MA: MIT Press, 2013.

Briggs, Mark. *Journalism Next: A Practical Guide to Digital Reporting and Publishing*. Washington, DC: CQ Press, 2010.

Gillmor, Dan. *We the Media: Grassroots Journalism by the People, for the People*. Sebastopol, CA: O'Reilly Media, 2008.

Hawthorne, Bobby. *The Radical Write: A Fresh Approach to Journalistic Writing for Students*, 3rd ed. Minneapolis, MN: Josten's, Inc., 2011.

Kaye, Jeff. *Funding Journalism in the Digital Age: Business Models, Strategies, Issues and Trends*. New York, NY: Peter Lang, 2010.

Luckie, Mark. *The Digital Journalist's Handbook*. Ebook. CreateSpace, 2011.

Mayor-Schonberger, Viktor, and Kenneth Cukier. *Big Data: A Revolution That Will Transform How We Live, Work, and Think*. New York, NY: Houghton Mifflin Harcourt, 2013.

Rosenberg, Scott. *Say Everything: How Blogging Began, What It's Becoming, and Why It Matters*. New York, NY: Crown Publishers, 2009.

Singer, P.W., and Allan Friedman. *Cybersecurity and Cyberwar: What Everyone Needs to Know*. Oxford, England: Oxford University, 2014.

Sites, Kevin. *In the Hot Zone: One Man, One Year, Twenty Wars*. New York, NY: Harper, 2007.

Stroud, Natalie. *Niche News: The Politics of News Choice*. New York, NY: Oxford, 2011.

END NOTES

[1] Watson, Frank. "Online Only News Site Wins Top Pulitzer Prize for Reporting." Searchenginewatch.com, 2011. Retrieved February 15, 2014 (http://searchenginewatch.com/article/2049700/Online-Only-News-Site-Wins-Top-Pulitzer-Prize-For-Reporting).

[2] Propublica.org. "About Us." Retrieved February 21, 2014 (http://www.propublica.org/about).

[3] Legrand, Roland. "Why Journalists Should Learn Computer Programming." PBS.org, 2010. Retrieved February 16, 2014 (http://www.pbs.org/mediashift/2010/06/why-journalists-should-learn-computer-programming153).

[4] Kaufman, Leslie. "New Owner of Patch Lays Off Hundreds." NYTimes.com, 2014. Retrieved February 22, 2014 (http://www.nytimes.com/2014/01/30/business/media/aols-struggling-patch-unit-has-more-layoffs.html?_r=0).

[5] Pew Research Center. "Overview." Retrieved February 22, 2014 (http://stateofthemedia.org/2013/overview-5).

[6] Green, Elizabeth. "The Continued Rise of Single-Subject Sites." Niemanlab.org, 2013. Retrieved February 22, 2014 (http://www.niemanlab.org/2013/12/the-continued-rise-of-single-subject-sites).

[7] Chalkbeat. "About Us." Retrieved February 21, 2014 (http://chalkbeat.org/#who).

[8] Smith, Dylan. "Getting Patched? Start Your Own News Site." Lionpublishers.com. Retrieved February 22, 2014 (http://www.lionpublishers.com/news/report/081513_patch).

[9] Tucsonsentinel.com. "Welcome to TucsonSentinel.com!" Retrieved February 22, 2014 (http://www.tucsonsentinel.com/about).

[10] LaBarre, Suzanne. "Why We're Shutting Off Our Comments." Popsci.com, 2013. Retrieved February 19, 2014 (http://www.popsci.com/science/article/2013-09/why-were-shutting-our-comments?dom=PSC&loc=recent&lnk=1&con=why-were-shutting-off-our-comments-).

END NOTES

[11] Statt, Nick. "Popular Science Silences Its Comments Section." CNET.com, 2013. Retrieved February 19, 2014 (http://news.cnet.com/8301-1023_3-57604412-93/popular-science-silences-its-comments-section).

[12] Muchnik, Lev, Sinan Aral, and Sean Taylor. "Social Influence Bias: A Randomized Experiment." Sciencemag.org, 2013. Retrieved February 19, 2014 (http://www.sciencemag.org/content/341/6146/647).

[13] Yoshida, Kate Shaw. "Online Comment Systems Reveal Multiple Layers of Social Bias." Arstechnica.com, 2013. Retrieved February 19, 2014 (http://arstechnica.com/science/2013/08/online-comment-systems-reveal-multiple-layers-of-social-bias).

[14] Cohn, Bob. "Comments on the Web: Engaging Readers or Swamping Journalism?" *Atlantic*, 2013. Retrieved February 19, 2014 (http://www.theatlantic.com/technology/archive/2013/08/comments-on-the-web-engaging-readers-or-swamping-journalism/278311).

[15] Devitt, Terry. "Trolls Win: Rude Comments Dim the Allure of Science Online." University of Wisconsin–Madison, 2013. Retrieved February 19, 2014 (http://www.news.wisc.edu/21506).

INDEX

A

aggregators, news, 4, 20, 33
AOL, 21

B

backpack journalists, 13–15
blogs, 4, 7, 9

C

Cameron, Darla, interview with, 16–19
Chalkbeat.org, 24–25
code/coders, 9–13
    need for journalists to learn code, 11–13
Cohn, Bob, 33–34
comments sections, for online stories, 30, 32–33, 38
    moderation of, 33–34
    and netiquette, 32–33
    up votes and down votes, 33

D

digital natives, 4, 5

F

forums, discussion, 30, 32–34

G

Green, Elizabeth, 24

H

Hale Global, 23
hyperlocal news, 20–26

J

journalists
    necessity of learning code, 11–13
    and online reader comments, 30, 34
    solo, 13–15

K

Kaiser Health News, 24

L

Lamothe, Dan, interview with, 35–38
linking stories online, 13
Local Independent Online News (LION), 26

M

media literacy, and understanding role of websites, 4–5

N

netiquette, 32–33
niche news, 24–25

O

online communities, challenges of, 30–34
online-only publications, 6–15

INDEX

P
Patch.com, 21–23, 26
Pew Research Center, 24
ProPublica, 7–9

S
Sites, Kevin, 13–15
Slate, 9
social media, 9, 30, 37
Statt, Nick, 33

T
traditional news websites, 4, 7, 9, 11, 20, 24
"trolls," 32
Truong, Doris, interview with, 27–29
TusconSentinel.com, 26

W
web developers, 9–11, 12

DIGITAL CONTENT CREATION

ABOUT THE AUTHOR

Megan Fromm is an assistant professor at Boise State University and faculty for the Salzburg Academy on Media & Global Change, a summer media literacy study-abroad program. She is also the professional support director for the Journalism Education Association.

Fromm received her Ph.D. in 2010 from the Philip Merrill College of Journalism at the University of Maryland. Her dissertation analyzed how news media frame student First Amendment court cases, particularly those involving freedom of speech and press. Her work and teaching centers on media law, scholastic journalism, media literacy, and media and democracy. She has also worked as a journalist and high school journalism teacher. Fromm has taught at Johns Hopkins University, Towson University, the University of Maryland, and the Newseum.

As a working journalist, Fromm won numerous awards, including the Society of Professional Journalists Sunshine Award and the Colorado Friend of the First Amendment Award. Fromm worked in student media through high school and college and interned at the Student Press Law Center in 2004. Her career in journalism began at Grand Junction High School (Grand Junction, Colorado), where she was a reporter and news editor for the award-winning student newspaper, the *Orange & Black*.

PHOTO CREDITS

Cover (hand with phone) © iStockphoto.com/Balavan; cover (phone screen image) © iStockphoto.com/cnythzl; cover (laptop) © iStockphoto.com/Adamo Di Loreto; cover (laptop monitor image) © iStockphoto.com/scyther5; cover (apps icons) © iStockphoto.com/scanrail; cover background (receding screens) © iStockphoto.com/Danil Melek; cover and interior pages (pixel pattern) © iStockphoto.com/hellena13; p. 5 Lionel Bonaventure/AFP/Getty Images; p. 7 Dan Ng/ProPublica/AP Images; p. 8 spaxiax/Shutterstock.com; pp. 10–11 © iStockphoto.com/ymgerman; p. 12 ahunjet/iStock/Thinkstock; pp. 14–15 Scott Peterson/Getty Images; p. 21 Paul J. Richards/AFP/Getty Images; pp. 22–23 Linda Whitwarn/Dorling Kindersley/Getty Images; p. 25 Joshua Hodge Photography/E+/Getty Images; p. 31 Marc Romanelli/Photographer's Choice/Getty Images; p. 32 blackred/E+/Getty Images.

Designer: Nicole Russo; Editor: Nicholas Croce; Photo Researcher: Karen Huang

Southern Lehigh Public Library
3200 Preston Lane
Center Valley, PA 18034